GAGARIN AND ARMSTRONG
The First Steps in Space

GAGARIN AND ARMSTRONG
The First Steps in Space

Clint Twist

RSVP

RAINTREE
STECK-VAUGHN
P U B L I S H E R S
The Steck-Vaughn Company

Austin, Texas

Published by Raintree Steck-Vaughn Publishers, an imprint of Steck-Vaughn Company

Series editor: Su Swallow
Editors: Nicola Barber, Shirley Shalit
Designer: Neil Sayer
Production: Jenny Mulvanny
Consultants: Ian Graham
                Gary E. Moulton, University of Nebraska—Lincoln
Illustrations: Richard Morris, Hardlines

Library of Congress Cataloging-in-Publication Data

Twist, Clint.
    Gagarin and Armstrong/ by Clint Twist.
        p.   cm. — (Beyond the horizons)
    Includes index.
    ISBN 0-8114-3978-X
    1. Astronautics — Soviet Union — History — Juvenile literature. 2. Astronautics — United States — History — Juvenile literature. 3. Outer space — Exploration — History — Juvenile literature. [1. Astronautics. 2. Outer space — Exploration.]
    I. Title. II. Series: Beyond the horizons.
    TL789.8.S65T88 1995
    919.9'04—dc20   94-32623
                                                CIP
                                                AC

Printed in Hong Kong

1 2 3 4 5 6 7 8 9 0 LB 99 98 97 96 95 94

This book is dedicated to the next generation and especially to Aimee, Bill, Ellen, Jack, Madeleine, Sophie, and Thomas.

Acknowledgments

For permission to reproduce copyright material the author and publishers gratefully acknowledge the following:
Cover (top left) John Sanford, Science Photo Library (middle left) NASA, Science Photo Library (bottom left) ZEFA (bottom right) Roger Ressmeyer, Science Photo Library
Title page NASA, Science Photo Library
page 4 (top) Hillary, Royal Geographical Society, (bottom) Hulton Deutsch Collection Limited **page 5** NASA, Science Photo Library **page 6** (left) Mary Evans Picture Library (right) Mercedes-Benz **page 7** (top) Mary Evans Picture Library, Alexander Meledin Collection (bottom) Hulton Deutsch Collection Limited **page 8** Mary Evans Picture Library, Alexander Meledin Collection **page 9** Hulton Deutsch Collection Limited **page 10** (top and bottom left) Mary Evans Picture Library (bottom right) David Parker, Science Photo Library **page 11** Science Photo Library **page 12** Hulton Deutsch Collection Limited **page 13** Hulton Deutsch Collection Limited **page 14** (left) J-L Charmet, Science Photo Library (right) Mary Evans Picture Library **page 15** Mary Evans Picture Library **page 16** (top) US Library of Congress, Science Photo Library (bottom) Mary Evans Picture Library **page 17** Richard Megna, Fundamental Photos, Science Photo Library **page 19** NASA, Science Photo Library **page 20** (top) Francois Gohier, Science Photo Library (bottom) Dr Eckart Pott, Bruce Coleman Limited **page 21** NASA, Science Photo Library **page 22** Novosti, Science Photo Library **page 23** (top) Hulton Deutsch Collection Limited (bottom) Novosti, Science Photo Library **page 24** Novosti, Science Photo Library **page 25** (top left and bottom) Novosti, Science Photo Library (top right) Hulton Deutsch Collection Limited **page 26** NASA, Science Photo Library **page 27** (top left) Arnie Sachs, Consolidated, Hulton (top right) NASA, Keystone Press Agency Ltd (bottom) NASA, Science Photo Library **page 28** NASA, Science Photo Library **page 29** NASA, Science Photo Library **page 30** (left) Roger Ressmeyer, Starlight, Science Photo Library (right) NASA, Science Photo Library **page 31** (top) Hulton Deutsch Collection Limited (bottom) Chris Alan Wilton, The Image Bank **page 32** (top) Earth Satellite Corporation, Science Photo Library (bottom left) Derek Berwin, The Image Bank (bottom right) NASA, Science Photo Library **page 33** (top) Sheila Terry, Rutherford Appleton Laboratory, Science Photo Library (bottom) NASA, Science Photo Library **page 35** (top) NASA, Science Photo Library (bottom) Roger Ressmeyer, Starlight, Science Photo Library **page 36** NASA, Science Photo Library **page 37** John Sanford, Science Photo Library **page 38** (left) Novosti, Science Photo Library (right) David P. Anderson SMU, NASA, Science Photo Library **page 39** NASA, Science Photo Library **page 40** (top) NASA, Science Photo Library (bottom) Hulton Deutsch Collection Limited **page 41** NASA, Science Photo Library **page 42** (top) NASA, Science Photo Library (bottom) Associated Press, Topham **page 43** (top) Topham Picture Source (bottom) NASA, Science Photo Library.

Contents

Introduction

Exploring planet Earth: Tenzing Norgay at the summit of Mount Everest, the highest mountain in the world, May 29, 1953. The photo was taken by his fellow climber, Edmund Hillary.

In 1961, the Russian cosmonaut Yuri Gagarin became the first person to travel through space. In 1969, the American astronaut Neil Armstrong became the first person to set foot on the moon. As a result of their achievements, Gagarin and Armstrong became world famous, and will probably remain famous for the rest of human history.

By the middle of the 20th century, human beings had thoroughly explored the planet upon which they evolved. They had climbed the highest mountain—Everest, 29,028 feet (8,848 m)—and descended to the ocean depths—Marianas Trench, 36,400 feet (11,034 m). All that remained was the conquest of space—the final frontier for human exploration.

The goals of space exploration were new discoveries and scientific knowledge. But one of the main motivations behind the conquest of space was the rivalry between two nations—the Soviet Union (as it was then) and the United States. These two nations were often known as "superpowers" because they were the two major powers in the world at the time. The rivalry between the Soviet Union and the United States created a "Space Race," in which the two superpowers raced against each other before a worldwide audience of billions for the glory of winning and being the first to put people into space.

Yuri Gagarin shortly after the flight that made him the first person to fly in space.

Neil Armstrong pictured a few hours before the launch of Apollo 11 to the moon.

Planet Earth rising above the surface of the moon. A member of the Apollo 11 crew took this photo.

Horizons

After reading this book you may want to find out more about Gagarin and Armstrong and the story of the first steps in space. At the end of some of the chapters, you will find **Horizons** boxes. These boxes contain the names of people and events that are not mentioned in this book but which are part of the story of space exploration. By looking up these names in the indexes of other reference books, you will discover still more fascinating information.

Both Russia and America had strong pioneering traditions. During the 18th and 19th centuries, while American pioneers moved into our huge western areas, Russian settlers moved eastward into Siberia. By the beginning of the 20th century, the pioneering was over, and the land was settled. Both nations, however, still had tremendous energy for exploration and expansion, and much of this energy became channeled into space research. Until 1957, human activity was confined to the Earth's atmosphere; by 1969, people were walking on the moon.

The Historical Background

The advance of technology in the 20th century. The Austin motorcar of 1911 was one of the first cars produced for the popular mass market. Note that the back seats can be removed for picnics! By contrast, the Mercedes is streamlined, and has a much more powerful engine, which is monitored by a small computer.

A century of change

In many respects, the history of the 20th century is one of unprecedented human progress. The speed of technological achievement and improvement has been amazing. We now take for granted many things, such as airplanes, television, computers, and cellular telephones, that within living memory were considered impossible dreams. Change has become the byword of the 20th century, and the pace of change has often been seemingly relentless. However, in 20th-century politics some things have remained remarkably unchanged, for example the way in which powerful nations create empires, which they then jealously guard and protect from all rivals.

At the beginning of the 20th century, much of the world was still controlled by the old colonial empires run from Europe. The most powerful European nations were Britain, France, and Germany. Although Germany was a relative newcomer to European politics, German steelworks and factories were the largest and most modern in the world. All three nations were allied by treaty to other countries. Britain and France were also allied against their main rival—Germany.

In August 1914, German armies attacked Belgium and France, which fought back supported strongly by Britain and Russia. The war soon spread beyond Europe, largely because of attacks on shipping. After four years of war, during which millions of people were killed or injured, Germany was eventually defeated. At 11 A.M. on November 11, 1918, the fighting stopped—World War I was over.

The Russian Revolution

World War I sparked off great changes in Russia. When Russia went to war against the Germans in 1914, the country was ruled by an emperor known as the czar. By 1917, the Russian armies had made little progress, and there was a great deal of discontent with the czar. What followed is known as the Russian Revolution, and the event is considered by many historians to mark the beginning of modern history.

A group of Russian revolutionaries pose with an armored car that they captured from the czar's army in October 1917.

The leaders of the Russian Revolution, Joseph Stalin (left) and Vladimir Ilyich Lenin (right).

The czar was overthrown and killed, and power was seized by a small group of people who followed the theories of the German political thinker, Karl Marx. These people were known as Communists. The leader of the Russian Communists was Vladimir Ilyich Lenin (1870–1924). He rewrote much of Marx's theory into what is now called Marxist-Leninism. One of his close associates was named Joseph Stalin (1879–1953). Stalin took over when Lenin died in 1924.

Lenin's government transformed Russia into the Union of Soviet Socialist Republics (USSR), also known as the Soviet Union. Many countries to the south of Russia were forced to become part of the USSR, and Russian was made the official language throughout the Soviet Union. Many people considered the USSR to be a Russian empire, and for this reason the word "Russian" is often used to describe people from all parts of the former Soviet Union.

The Soviet state

Lenin and Stalin soon discovered that it was necessary to use force to encourage Soviet citizens to cooperate in creating a Communist state. Countless millions of peasants, ordinary

Karl Marx

Karl Marx (1818–83) wrote two very influential books. One was *Das Kapital* (*Capital*), an analysis of industrial society. The other book, cowritten with Friedrich Engels (1820–95), was *The Manifesto of the Communist Party*. Marx was concerned with the plight of poor working-class people. He believed that the working classes were exploited by the rich ruling classes and that political power should be exercised by the workers rather than by rich land or factory owners. In a Communist state (organized according to Marxist principles), property such as factories, farms, and houses would not be owned privately, but would belong to the state. The state was to be controlled by a central government elected by the workers. Marx believed that this was the only way to create a society in which people would not be oppressed by inequalities of background. In a Marxist state, everybody would be equal—that was the theory.

people who wanted no more than a small patch of land on which to grow their own food, were forced to move onto huge collective farms. These farms were told what to grow by the government. Anyone who refused to cooperate was left to starve. Between 1920 and 1940, about ten million Soviet citizens died as a result of the collective farm system.

The Communists became obsessed with bringing the Soviet Union up to date. Russia had been an agricultural country when Lenin took power. Under Stalin, factories were built to try to rival those of Germany, Britain, and the United States. The only way this could be done was by exercising a great deal of control over the lives of the population. The Soviet state could only succeed if the government told people exactly what to do all the time. The idea of free elections quickly disappeared. There were elections, but all the candidates were chosen by the Communist Party. There was no right of free speech or religious worship. Anyone who spoke out against the Communist government was sent to a prison camp to work as slave labor. People lived in constant fear of the government's secret police.

Distribution of the food ration on a Soviet collective farm during the 1920s, a time of severe shortages in Russia.

Adolf Hitler (standing in the car) salutes his party supporters as they march through the streets of a German town in 1927.

Hitler's Germany

In Germany, a Communist revolution was attempted after World War I, but it failed. Instead, an elected government was installed.

During the 1920s, the German economy collapsed because of worldwide economic problems. Many Germans began to support a political party founded by a man named Adolf Hitler. Hitler made himself popular by blaming Germany's problems on other countries, and by promising to get rid of foreign workers. Through skillful use of new methods of mass communication, such as radio and film, Hitler was able to convince many Germans that they had a special place in the world. In 1933, Hitler was appointed Chancellor of Germany, and he quickly made himself dictator (absolute ruler). Like the Communists in the USSR, Hitler used secret police to control the lives of ordinary citizens.

In 1939, Hitler sent German armies to invade Poland, knowing that this would lead to war with Britain and France. Using tanks and bomber aircraft, German armies soon occupied most of western Europe. Two years later, Hitler attacked the Soviet Union.

On December 7, 1941, Japan took advantage of the European war and attacked the United States, intending to take control of most of the Pacific region. The U.S. entered the war to fight against Germany and Japan. By May 1945 a combination of British and American armies in the West and Soviet armies in the East had defeated Germany. Hitler killed himself as Soviet troops entered Berlin, the capital of Germany.

Although they were losing the war, the Japanese continued to fight fiercely in the Pacific. On August 6, 1945, an American warplane dropped an atomic bomb on the city of Hiroshima, and three days later another bomb on the city of Nagasaki. Japan surrendered immediately; World War II was over.

Scientific progress

Throughout history, warfare has always stimulated scientific and technical progress. By the end of World War II, many important new technologies had become firmly established and were poised for further development.

Radio The use of radio waves had been pioneered by the Italian inventor Guglielmo Marconi (1874–1937), who sent the first radio signals across the Atlantic Ocean in 1901. Commercial radio broadcasting began in the 1920s, and the technology of television was developed. During the 1930s, the first experimental television programs were transmitted, although very few people had television sets.

During World War II, radar was developed. Radar was used to locate distant objects by listening to the echoes from a "beam" of invisible radio waves. By the end of the war, radar could be used to follow the movement of individual aircraft in flight. More powerful radar equipment could track objects in space.

Computers Until the 19th century, the only "adding machines" were ancient inventions such as the abacus. In 1812, the British mathematician Charles Babbage had invented a calculating machine that used a series of toothed wheels, but it was not a great success.

During World War II, the first electronic calculating machines were built. They could do the work of a whole roomful of mathematicians. These first machines were designed in order to

Guglielmo Marconi won the 1909 Nobel Prize for Physics for the invention of radio transmission.

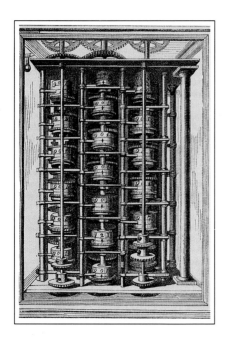

Babbage's mechanical calculating machine (above). This illustration is from an 1854 encyclopedia.

This modern supercomputer can electronically store the equivalent of 128 million words (the equivalent of 10,000 books like this one).

decode enemy secret messages. One of the people involved in this work was the British mathematician, Alan Turing. In 1936 he put forward the idea of a "universal" electronic machine that would follow whatever instructions it was given. The computer as we know it today had been born.

Aircraft At the beginning of World War II, all the world's aircraft were powered by piston engines that turned propellers. Some were monoplanes (with one set of wings), but many were biplanes like the Wright brothers' original design (with two wings, one above the other; see page 16). The fastest monoplanes of the time reached speeds of just over 400 miles (700 km) per hour, and they could not fly higher than about 13,000 feet (4,000 m). By the end of the war, the first jet aircraft were flying. These aircraft would eventually fly faster than 1,800 miles (3,000 km) per hour and reach heights of more than 115,000 feet (35,000 m).

Even more exciting was another wartime development, the German A4 rocket (sometimes called the V2). Produced by a team of scientists, of whom the most famous is Werner von Braun (1912–77), the A4 was designed to carry one ton of explosive to cities hundreds of miles away. The A4 was the first guided missile, and on its journey of destruction it passed out of the Earth's atmosphere (see page 15). The first space vehicle had been invented.

Atomic power Atoms are the basic units of the chemical elements that make up matter. Everything, living and nonliving,

A false-color photo of the mushroom cloud produced by the explosion of an atomic bomb. The size of the explosion is indicated by the ships nearby.

is made up of atoms of different elements. Scientists first began to explore the secrets of the atom toward the end of the 19th century. Among the early pioneers was the Polish scientist Marie Curie (1867–1934) who, in partnership with her husband, Pierre, discovered the radioactive element radium. Radioactivity is a form of energy produced naturally by a few elements. According to the theories of the German-American mathematician Albert Einstein (1879–1955), it is possible to release the energy contained in radioactive elements. The energy can be released slowly, inside an atomic reactor; or quickly to produce an atomic explosion. During the 1930s, scientists in several countries investigated the possibilities of an atomic reactor to produce useful energy. But after World War II started, the emphasis of research switched to the development of a powerful bomb. After the United States entered the war, American scientists began work on the top-secret Manhattan Project to make an atomic bomb ("A-bomb"). On July 16, 1945, they tested the first atomic bomb in the desert of New Mexico. Less than 220 pounds (100 kg) of the radioactive element uranium produced a huge explosion. The atom bomb proved to be many thousands of times more powerful than ordinary explosives.

Into the atomic age

World War II completely altered the political map of Europe. Stalin refused to release any of the territory that Soviet armies had captured during the war. The other victorious countries, Britain, France, and the United States, were too exhausted by war to oppose Stalin. Britain and France wanted to concentrate on rebuilding their damaged towns and cities, as well as solving the long-term problem of what to do with their overseas empires. The U.S. was reluctant to act alone.

Eastern Europe was now a part of the Soviet empire. Some occupied countries were allowed to keep their national boundaries; others were simply absorbed into the Soviet Union. Communist governments were installed and free elections were not permitted. Any opposition to Communist rule was ruthlessly crushed by force. The dividing line between Communist and non-Communist Europe became known as the "Iron Curtain." This situation remained frozen for more than 40 years because there was an important new factor in world politics—the atomic bomb.

The power of the atomic bomb had shocked the whole world. A single A-bomb the size of a small car could destroy an entire city. More than 50,000 people died in an instant at Hiroshima, and about the same number at Nagasaki. In 1945, only America had this awesome new weapon, but military leaders in several countries were quick to see the possibilities of combining the atomic bomb with the guided missile (see page 11). A single missile could destroy a whole city; a hundred missiles could destroy a whole country.

America shared the secret of making atomic bombs with Britain and France, and could not prevent the Soviet Union from developing its own atomic weapons. By the mid-1950s, the U.S. and the USSR both had long-range missiles tipped with thermonuclear bombs that were even more powerful than atomic bombs. Thermonuclear bombs are also known as hydrogen bombs ("H-bombs").

A Russian soldier hoists the Soviet flag above the ruins of Hitler's Berlin at the end of World War II.

The city of Hiroshima after being hit by an atomic bomb. Entire city blocks were destroyed, and only a few concrete buildings survived the explosion.

Horizons

You could find out about the following people who all have a place in the history of the years leading up to the first steps in space: Count Ferdinand von Zeppelin (German airship designer); Henry Ford (American industrialist); Benito Mussolini (Italian leader and friend of Adolf Hitler); Jesse Owens (American Olympic medal winner); Winston Churchill (British leader during World War II); Nikita Khrushchev (leader of USSR); Dwight Eisenhower (American President).

At the end of World War II, the United States, Britain, and France remained allied because they were opposed to the Soviet occupation of Eastern Europe, and to the further expansion of communism. Many other countries, in Europe and elsewhere, also joined this alliance against the Soviet empire. But the United States was by far the strongest member of the anti-Soviet alliance, and world politics became dominated by the rivalry between the two "superpowers," the U.S. and the USSR.

The power of the A-bomb and the H-bomb meant that neither side could risk all-out war. Both the Russians and the Americans were acting according to the theory that neither side would attack the other with nuclear missiles because they knew that the other side's missiles would in turn destroy them. This situation produced what was called the "balance of terror." According to the reasoning of this theory, the world was actually a safer place because of the atomic bomb.

Prevented by fear from engaging in all-out war with one another, the two sides found other ways of fighting what became known as the "Cold War." One way was to compete for scientific and technological achievement. The most exciting aspect of this scientific competition was the Space Race, which began in 1957 when the Soviet Union launched the first artificial satellite into orbit around the Earth.

The Technology of Transportation

Exploring space

Until the middle of the 20th century, human exploration of space was limited to what could be seen from Earth. The apparent movement of the sun across the sky had long provided natural units of time (the day and year) around which people could organize their lives. The phases of the moon provided another less accurate unit, the month. The patterns made by stars in the night sky (constellations) also fascinated early peoples, and they gave names to the most obvious ones. Because of their viewpoint on Earth, people naturally thought that the sun, moon, planets, and stars all revolved around the Earth.

During the 16th and 17th centuries, a series of discoveries changed people's view of the world in which they lived. Ocean explorers such as Ferdinand Magellan (1480–1521) proved beyond doubt that the world was round, like a ball. The invention of the telescope enabled astronomers to get a closer look at the stars and planets, and by measuring their movements in the sky, astronomers were able to develop a new picture of space that was very different from the traditional view.

According to the new picture, the Earth and a number of other planets, including Mercury, Venus, Mars, Jupiter, and Saturn, traveled through space in near-circular orbits around the sun. The moon traveled in orbit around the Earth. Other planets, such as Jupiter and Saturn, also had their own orbiting moons. The stars were much farther away, and only appeared to move because of the spinning of the Earth on its axis. At first there was much opposition to these new, revolutionary ideas, but slowly they were accepted.

The traditional view, which was supported by the Church, placed the Earth at the center of the universe.

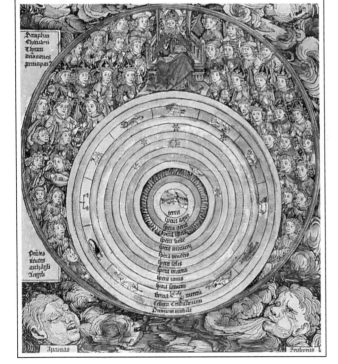

The new picture of the universe (right), taken from an 18th-century star atlas. The sun is at the center of the solar system and the moon is shown orbiting the Earth.

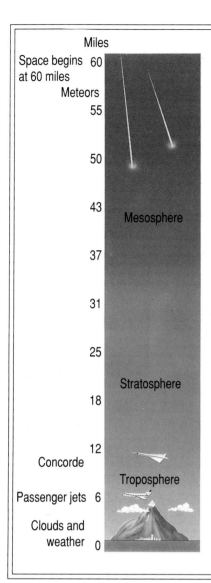

Miles
Space begins 60
at 60 miles
Meteors
55

50

43
Mesosphere

37

31

25
Stratosphere
18

12
Concorde
Troposphere
Passenger jets 6

Clouds and
weather 0

The Earth's Atmosphere

The Earth is surrounded by a 60-mile (100-km) deep layer of gases known as the atmosphere. The atmosphere, which we call air, consists mainly of nitrogen (77 percent) and oxygen (21 percent) together with small amounts of carbon dioxide, water vapor, and a few other gases. The oxygen in the atmosphere is essential to life. Apart from some types of microorganisms, all living things need a constant supply of oxygen in order to remain alive.

However, the Earth's atmosphere does far more than supply living things with oxygen. The atmosphere acts like a giant pair of sunglasses, absorbing most of the harmful radiation in sunlight. Without the atmosphere filtering the sun's rays, the ultraviolet (UV) radiation in sunlight would make life as we know it on Earth almost impossible. The atmosphere also acts as a giant blanket, keeping warmth in and preventing the Earth's surface from getting too cold at night.

The gases in the atmosphere are most concentrated at the Earth's surface. Rising away from the surface, the air gets thinner and thinner. Above about 33,000 feet (10,000 m), the air is too thin for humans to breathe normally, and to travel higher requires special breathing equipment. The weight of the atmosphere pressing down on the surface of the Earth produces what is known as atmospheric pressure. As the air gets thinner at higher altitudes, atmospheric pressure decreases. Once again, the limit of human endurance is at about 33,000 feet above the Earth. Aircraft that travel above this height have to provide a pressurized environment for passengers and crew.

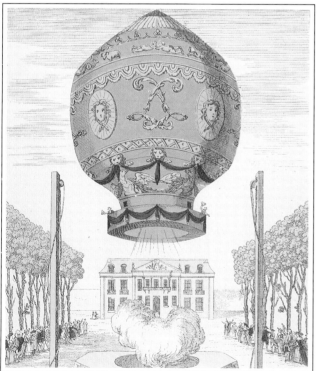

First flights

The first people known to have defeated gravity and risen from the ground were the French brothers Joseph and Jacques Montgolfier, who in 1783 first "flew" in a hot-air balloon. The air trapped inside the balloon was heated by a small fire. The hot air was lighter than the air surrounding the balloon, and so the balloon lifted off the ground. In the 19th century, balloons filled with lighter-than-air gases, such as hydrogen, were developed. Balloons, however, had several limitations: they were difficult to steer and were very vulnerable to bad weather.

Joseph and Jacques Montgolfier wave to the crowds during their first successful balloon flight.

15

The first flight by a powered aircraft, December 17, 1903, piloted by Orville Wright. The aircraft reached a maximum height of 11.5 feet (3.5 m).

Toward the end of the century, scientists and inventors started thinking about other means of achieving the dream of flight. On December 17, 1903, the American brothers Wilbur and Orville Wright tested the world's first heavier-than-air flying machine near Kitty Hawk in North Carolina. The first flight, with Orville as pilot, lasted just 12 seconds and covered 120 feet (36.5 m). Later the same day, a 59-second flight covered a distance of about 855 feet (260 m).

Within two years the Wright brothers had perfected their aircraft and achieved a 38-minute flight, traveling more than 25 miles (40 km). They toured abroad promoting their invention and soon gained worldwide fame. People in many different countries took up the challenge of flying.

Aircraft developed rapidly, and were used widely during World War I. After World War I, the first aircraft passenger services began in Europe and the United States, and by the mid-1930s international air travel was well-established. World War II brought further developments and introduced the jet engine.

From the point of view of space research, however, aircraft were of only limited use. The engines that powered aircraft, both piston engines and jets, required air in which to work. These air-breathing engines were perfectly suited to conditions near the Earth's surface, but of no use at heights of more than 25 miles above the Earth. Exploring space meant using rockets.

In-flight comfort from a 1936 air travel brochure.

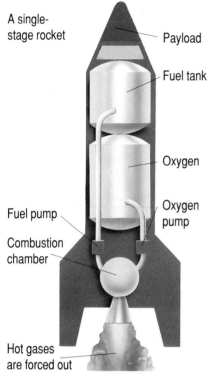

A single-stage rocket

Payload

Fuel tank

Oxygen

Fuel pump

Oxygen pump

Combustion chamber

Hot gases are forced out

Rockets

A rocket is powered by a slow explosion inside a tube that is closed at one end and open at the other. Hot gases produced by the explosion leave the open end of the tube, producing a force that pushes the tube in the opposite direction. The simplest rocket is the gunpowder rocket, or firework, that was invented by the Chinese more than 1,000 years ago, and is still used as part of celebrations all over the world. But for a rocket to overcome the Earth's gravity and enter space requires a much more powerful fuel than gunpowder.

The first person to think seriously about using rockets for space exploration was a Russian mathematician, Konstantin Tsiolkovsky (1857–1935). In 1895, he wrote a scientific article in which he proposed using a multi-stage rocket powered by liquid fuel instead of gunpowder. The stages would burn in sequence, each stage pushing the rocket faster before it burned out. His paper attracted little attention, and his work was soon forgotten.

During the 1920s, the American scientist Robert Goddard (1882–1945) experimented with rockets, and in 1926 he successfully launched a small rocket powered by liquid fuel. Although the rocket rose less than 49 feet (15 m) into the air, it proved that some of Tsiolkovsky's ideas had been correct. However, there was not much more research into rockets until World War II, when rockets were developed to bombard cities.

After World War II, the development of bigger and more powerful rockets became a priority as the two superpowers built up their stocks of missiles. The most powerful rockets were known as Inter-Continental Ballistic Missiles (ICBMs), and could carry a nuclear bomb to a target 6,000 miles (10,000 km) away. In both the U.S. and the USSR, some scientists realized that ICBMs could be adapted to carry scientific instruments, and perhaps even people, deep into space.

A typical ICBM had three stages. The first two stages consisted entirely of rocket motors and fuel tanks. The third stage carried the payload (usually an H-bomb) and the equipment to guide the missile. The first stage had the most powerful motors, and usually had extra booster rockets attached to the side. This stage lifted the rocket off the launch pad and up into the atmosphere. After the boosters had used up their fuel, they dropped away. The first stage engine continued to lift the rocket skyward until it too ran out of fuel, and fell back to Earth. The second stage engines then ignited, increasing the rocket's speed. When they had used up their fuel, the second stage fell away while the third stage delivered the payload.

Fireworks rockets, fueled by gunpowder, explode in midair to produce brightly colored effects.

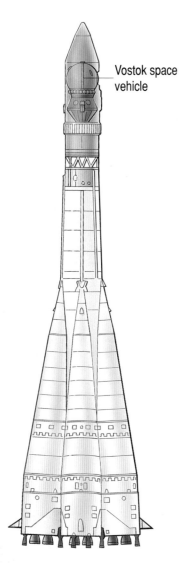

Vostok space
vehicle

The Vostok rocket

The rocket used to launch Yuri Gagarin into space in 1961 was 125 feet (38 m) tall. The first stage, which measured 79 feet (24 m), contained eight rocket engines with four additional boosters, each containing six engines. All 32 rockets in the first stage were used for the launch. The Vostok space vehicle in which Gagarin sat weighed less than five tons.

The Saturn V rocket, which eight years later launched Neil Armstrong and his companions on their way to the moon, was much larger. The rocket stood 366 feet (111 m) tall, and when fully fueled weighed nearly 3,000 tons. There were three rocket stages, and the Saturn V could lift the equivalent of 30 Vostok space vehicles off the ground and into space.

Earth orbit

The first goal of the new space scientists was to place a spacecraft in orbit around the Earth. Orbit is a naturally stable relationship between two objects moving in space. If one object is much larger than the other, then the small object will orbit around the larger. If the objects are of similar size, they will both orbit around a point somewhere in between them.

In order to place a spacecraft in orbit, scientists knew that the rocket driving the craft must be powerful enough to overcome the pull of the Earth's gravity. At heights above 60 miles (100 km), the pull of gravity is much weaker, but an object will still fall back to Earth. So a rocket has to be traveling fast enough to stay in orbit—about 17,000 miles (28,000 km) per hour. This is the orbital velocity, when the speed of the object counters the pull of gravity and the object remains in "free fall" around the Earth. In free fall, objects have no weight and "float" in space. They are often said to be "weightless."

Objects in orbit around a planet are called satellites. The Earth has a natural satellite—the moon—which orbits at a distance of about 222,000 miles (370,000 km). The idea of artificial satellites had been suggested some years before space exploration became possible. In the 1940s, the British writer Arthur C. Clarke suggested that artificial satellites could be placed in geostationary orbits, remaining above the same point on the Earth's surface. Such satellites could be used to relay radio signals around the world. Satellites could also be used to take scientific measurements in space, or even to look down on the Earth. One of the achievements of the Space Race was to turn such ideas into realities.

Radio communication was absolutely essential for the exploration of space. Even the simplest radio transmitter on board a satellite enabled scientists back on Earth to keep track of its position in orbit. More complex radio equipment could send back information from scientific equipment. After human spaceflight began, radio allowed the occupants of a space vehicle to remain in contact with mission control on Earth throughout their space flight.

The Moon

For thousands of years people have gazed up and studied the moon, gradually learning more about our nearest neighbor in space. Because of the moon's own rotation, only one side is ever visible from Earth, the other side, known as the dark side, is permanently turned away.

The moon is a barren, rocky world about one-fifth the volume of Earth, and one-quarter its diameter. By measuring the size of the moon, scientists were able to calculate that its gravity was only about 17 percent of Earth's gravity. Unlike Earth, the moon does not have an atmosphere, so its surface is unprotected from the harsh environment of space. The lack of atmosphere around the moon also means that there is no air for people to breathe, and a wide range of temperatures between day and night.

The moon, photographed from the Apollo 11 rocket.

Surviving space

Exploring space required much greater preparation than any other feat of human exploration. Space was a new environment for human beings that could not be endured without special breathing apparatus. There was also the danger of meteoroids, pieces of natural rock and metal traveling through space that range in size from dust particles to small houses. When meteoroids collide with a moon or planet, they are known as meteorites. The surface of the moon is covered by craters made by the impact of meteorites. However, most meteorites that reach the Earth burn up in its atmosphere, producing streaks of light called meteors. So, at first, scientists had no real idea how many meteoroids there were in space, or how much protection a space vehicle would

A 2,640-foot-(800-m) wide meteorite crater in Arizona. The crater was made by a meteorite that hit the Earth about 50,000 years ago.

need. There was also the problem of radiation. The Earth's atmosphere shields our planet from most of the harmful radiation coming from the sun and elsewhere in space. Once above the atmosphere, a space vehicle and its occupants would be exposed to unknown quantities of radiation.

As a result of the Cold War, all these problems were faced by two rival teams of scientists and engineers. Instead of combining their research, the space exploration teams in the United States and the USSR worked independently, often in conditions of utmost secrecy. In fact, the rival teams dealt with the problems of space travel in much the same way, and the equipment and vehicles they produced looked remarkably alike.

Experience with satellites showed that space vehicles did not need heavy armor against meteoroids, so spacecraft designed to carry human beings could be reasonably lightweight. However, any spacecraft returning to Earth did need protection from the atmosphere; otherwise it would burn up just like a meteor. This problem was solved by attaching a thick layer of heat-resistant material, a heat shield, to one end.

The largest meteorite yet discovered weighs 55 tons and was found in southwest Africa.

Carrying people to the moon and back required the most complex space vehicle ever built. The Saturn V rocket had three stages, and the Apollo space vehicle was also made up of three separate units, called modules. The service module contained the rocket motor to drive the craft from Earth orbit to the moon and back. It also carried the life-support system that kept the crew

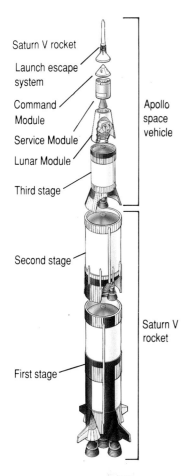

Saturn V rocket

Launch escape system

Command Module

Service Module

Lunar Module

Third stage

Apollo space vehicle

Second stage

Saturn V rocket

First stage

Horizons

You could find out about the following people who all made a contribution to astronomy—the study of objects in space as seen from Earth: Ptolemy (proposed the ancient theory that the sun, planets, and stars orbit the Earth); Nicolaus Copernicus (established that the Earth orbits the sun); Galileo Galilei (discovered the rings around Saturn); Isaac Newton (invented the reflecting telescope); Edmund Halley (showed that comets also orbit the sun); Edwin Hubble (proved the existence of other galaxies).

alive. The command module was only 10 feet (3m) long. This was where the crew spent most of the voyage. The command module was pressurized and supplied with air, and was the only part of the space vehicle to return to Earth. The lunar module was itself in two parts (the word *lunar* means "of the moon"). Both parts descended to the moon's surface, but only the upper part returned to lunar orbit. The lower part was left behind. Altogether, the three modules of the Apollo craft measured 59 feet (18 m) in length, and weighed 44 tons.

Crews and training

Space vehicles needed human crews, unless the exploration of space was to be carried out by robots and animals. Both the USSR and the United States chose military test pilots to take the first rides into space.

The Russians called their space travelers cosmonauts and the Americans called theirs astronauts, but there the difference ended. Both sets of crews were fit young men (and later on women) who were experienced at operating complicated machinery while flying at high speed. To prepare them for the experience of a rocket launch, the trainee space travelers were subjected to extreme physical stress while they were monitored by medical instruments. They were spun around by powerful motors, and strapped into rocket sleds that were fired along rails. Anyone who was even slightly unfit had to drop out.

As the exploration of space progressed, more complex training was carried out based on the experiences of the first cosmonauts and astronauts. Trainees practiced carrying out tasks underwater to imitate the conditions of weightlessness. In the United States, astronaut training was soon opened to civilian volunteers, and many scientists and engineers became astronauts. The Soviet Union relied more on military cosmonauts. Both superpowers also trained a few people from other countries and launched them into space as crew members.

American military test pilots. Neil Armstrong is second from the left.

Yuri Gagarin's Voyage into Space

First steps

Preparations for Yuri Gagarin's voyage into space started in the late 1940s, when Gagarin himself was still in high school. After the end of World War II, Soviet engineers began building improved versions of the A4 rocket (see page 11) based on designs taken from Germany. At first, all their efforts were put into the development of ICBMs, but in 1949 Soviet scientists began to explore space. Rockets carrying scientific instruments were sent high into Earth's atmosphere to measure conditions there. During the 1950s, small animals such as dogs and monkeys were put into specially designed pressure suits and sent on ten-minute trips to the edge of space. During these tests, instruments and film cameras recorded the effects of short periods of weightlessness on the animals.

Messenger in orbit

In 1957, President Eisenhower announced that the United States would put an artificial satellite into orbit around the Earth as part of an international research program. The satellite was to be launched some time the following year.

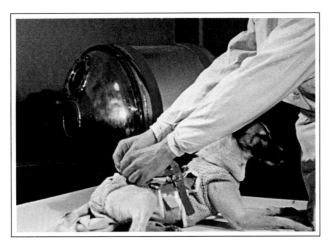

A technician prepares Laika for her journey into space which, sadly, was to be one-way only.

On October 4, 1957, Russian news services shocked the world when they announced that a Soviet rocket had launched Sputnik 1, the world's first artificial satellite. As people all over the world listened to the "beep beep" signal transmitted by radio equipment aboard Sputnik 1, they realized that the Russians had won an important victory. Although the "beep beep" from space was meaningless in any language, the satellite did indeed carry a message—the USSR had beaten the United States to be the first into space. Sputnik continued to orbit the Earth for 92 days until it fell into the atmosphere and burned up.

Soviet scientists pressed on with the exploration of space. A month after the success of Sputnik 1, they launched another satellite, Sputnik 2, this time containing a dog, the first Earth creature ever to travel in space. The "space dog," named Laika, remained in orbit for several days before her oxygen ran out and she died.

In October 1959, the Soviet Union launched a rocket that escaped Earth's gravity completely, and carried a satellite into orbit around the moon. Cameras aboard the satellite sent back the first images of the dark side of the moon, the side that cannot be seen from Earth. By the beginning of the 1960s, Soviet ICBMs were powerful enough to lift a five-ton space vehicle into orbit.

At the secret Baikonur base in southern Russia, engineers and scientists began preparing for the launch of Vostok—the space vehicle that would carry the first human being into space.

Yuri Gagarin

Yuri Gagarin during cosmonaut training.

The launch of Vostok 1, which carried Yuri Gagarin on his historic voyage into space.

Yuri Gagarin was born on March 9, 1934, near the town of Gzhatsk, just west of Moscow. His home was on a collective farm where his father worked as a carpenter. In May 1941, when he was seven years old, young Yuri started school. Two weeks later, at the beginning of June, German armies invaded Russia. His father joined the army, and his mother took Yuri and his older brother and sister away from the fighting. After the war was over, they returned to Gzhatsk, and Yuri resumed his schooling.

He decided to train as a technician, and attended a technical school on the outskirts of Moscow. He left school in 1951 as a trained metalworker and enrolled at an industrial college. While he was a student, he became interested in aircraft and took lessons at a local flying school. Gagarin discovered that he loved flying, and abandoned his plans to become a technician. Instead, when he graduated from college in 1955, he joined the Soviet air force and became a pilot.

Yuri Gagarin had a natural talent for flying, and his abilities were soon noticed. He was taken off normal duties and became a test pilot, flying new and experimental aircraft. Gagarin was such a good test pilot that he was selected to "pilot" the first space vehicle —Vostok 1. After selection, he was given special training to prepare him for this historic voyage.

First man in space

At 9:07A.M. (local time in southern Russia) on April 12, 1961, powerful rocket motors ignited, and Flight Major Gagarin was hurled vertically upward into the sky. At 10:55A.M., he was back on the ground, having made a single orbit and traveled more than 24,000 miles (40,000 km). In less than two hours—108 minutes to be exact—Gagarin had circled the globe. At the farthest point of his orbit, he had reached a height of 196 miles (327 km) above the Earth's surface, and the Vostok space vehicle had reached a maximum speed of 16,956 miles (28,260 km) per hour.

The path of Vostok's orbit took Gagarin over most of the inhabited world, and he was able to see signs of human activity as well as natural features, such as rivers and coastlines. As he traveled over the Soviet Union, Gagarin could see the great rectangular fields of collective farms. Gagarin also became the first person to talk to the Earth from space by radio. During his flight he

The Vostok 1 descent module landed safely back on Earth.

kept the scientists on the ground informed of what was happening. While passing over Africa, he was able to report, "I am withstanding the effects of weightlessness well."

At the end of the orbit, Gagarin climbed out of his seat in the Vostok vehicle and crawled into the ball-shaped reentry module, which then separated from Vostok and fell back to Earth. Once the reentry module was safely back inside the Earth's atmosphere, Gagarin descended by parachute to the ground. The first space traveler had returned.

Soviet success

The Soviet news services were triumphant—once again the USSR had beaten the United States with an important "first step" into space. The success of his space flight made Gagarin instantly famous, and he was presented to the world as an ideal hero of the Soviet Union. He was a young man from an ordinary background who had been trained by the Soviet state to become the first "spaceman." For a year or so after his flight, Gagarin made a series of visits to various countries, including India, Egypt, Canada, Brazil, and Britain, as a spokesman for the Soviet space program. He also attended international conferences about spaceflight. Everywhere he went, he was given a hero's welcome.

The official Russian celebration of Gagarin's flight in Red Square, Moscow.

Soviet space scientists were quick to follow up their success with a series of Vostok vehicles. In August 1961, the cosmonaut Gherman Titov made 17 orbits of the Earth inside Vostok 2, and a year later cosmonaut Andrian Nikolayev completed 64 orbits aboard Vostok 3. In June 1963, Valentina Tereshkova became the first woman in space, when she completed a total of 48 orbits around the Earth. Meanwhile another cosmonaut had pushed the number of Earth orbits to 81, a space voyage that lasted four days.

Valentina Tereshkova (above) emerging from the spacecraft in which she orbited the earth 48 times in June 1963.

The first space walk (right). Tethered by a lifeline, cosmonaut Alexei Leonov floats in open space more than 60 miles (100 km) above the Earth's surface.

In October 1964, the Russians launched the first multi-crew space vehicle, Voskhod 1, with three cosmonauts aboard, including one who was a doctor. In March 1965, Voskhod 2 was launched with two crew members aboard. While orbiting the Earth, cosmonaut Alexei Leonov climbed out of the space vehicle, tethered by a lifeline but unprotected except for his spacesuit. Until this first "spacewalk," human travelers in space had remained inside their pressurized vehicles, their spacesuits for use only in emergencies. The voyage of Voskhod 2 proved that it was possible for people to work in space.

Throughout the 1960s, Yuri Gagarin was in charge of the Soviet cosmonaut training program. But he longed to return to space, and was preparing for another possible space flight when, on March 27, 1968, he took off on a routine test flight. The aircraft crashed and Gagarin was killed.

The race to the moon

Soviet heroes, Gagarin and Tereshkova, the first man and woman in space.

By the late 1960s, Soviet scientists were working toward landing the first people on the moon. In 1966, they launched Luna 9, which made the first successful "soft" landing on the moon. "Soft" means that rockets were used to slow the vehicle so that the equipment aboard was not damaged by the landing—an important first step if people were to land safely. They also launched a series of robot Zond vehicles that orbited the moon, then returned to Earth. At the beginning of 1969, the Soviets were nearly ready to send a crew of cosmonauts to orbit the moon. But by then the U.S. had overtaken the USSR in the Space Race. In mid-1969, the United States landed astronauts on the moon.

Neil Armstrong's Voyage to the Moon

The first Americans selected for astronaut training posed in their newly designed spacesuits. Alan Shepard is in the back row, left. John Glenn is third from the left in the front row.

Alan Shepard being hoisted aboard a helicopter at the end of the flight that made him the first American in space.

Starting in second place

American scientists were planning their own artificial satellite when they were overtaken by the success of the Soviet Sputnik. An American Vanguard satellite was hurriedly launched in December 1957, but the rocket burst into flames instead of soaring into space. The U.S. did not successfully launch a satellite until January 1958, when Explorer 1 was put into orbit.

American plans for the human exploration of space also lagged behind the Russians at first. U.S. scientists were still investigating the possibility of sending someone on a sub-orbital "hop" into space when Yuri Gagarin took the first orbital ride around the world in April 1961. The following month the first American astronaut, Alan Shepard, made a brief up-and-down trip aboard a Mercury space vehicle that reached a height of 110 miles (185 km) before safely splashing down in the sea. Eleven weeks later, Virgil "Gus" Grissom made a similar "space-hop." On February 20, 1962, the Americans finally launched an astronaut into orbit. Traveling inside another Mercury vehicle, John Glenn became the first American in orbit.

Target—the moon

The Americans had more ambitious plans than merely catching up with the Russians. In May 1961 President John F. Kennedy announced that America would aim to put people on the moon by the end of the 1960s. Cape Canaveral in Florida was established as the main launching site for U.S. space rockets.

A new series of Gemini space vehicles was designed and built, each of which could carry two astronauts. In 1966, a Gemini vehicle linked up with a robot vehicle while in orbit and completed the first space-docking. Space-docking proved that vehicles could be maneuvered very precisely while they were in space, which would be essential on a journey to the moon and back.

Meanwhile, a series of Orbiter satellites were sent to the moon to photograph possible landing sites. The high quality photographs sent back by the Orbiters provided the scientists with their first

President John F. Kennedy, who committed America to putting a man on the moon before the end of the 1960s.

One of the photographs taken by the American Orbiter satellites during their search for a suitable landing place on the moon.

The crew of Apollo 11 (left to right, Collins, Armstrong, and Aldrin) photographed after their historic flight.

really detailed look at the moon's surface. Later, a series of Surveyor robot probes were launched to make soft landings on the moon. Information sent back by the Surveyors helped the engineers design the space vehicle that would actually land on the moon's surface.

Within a few years of President John F. Kennedy's announcement, American engineers had enough information to build the Apollo space vehicle, which was designed to carry three people on a return journey to the moon. To be successful, the different parts of the Apollo vehicle had to separate and rejoin at exactly the right times. Each stage of the journey was carefully rehearsed. In July 1969, Apollo 11 was ready for its historic journey to the moon. The crew chosen for the Apollo vehicle were experienced astronauts Edwin "Buzz" Aldrin, Michael Collins, and Neil Armstrong.

Neil Armstrong

Neil Armstrong was born on August 5, 1930, at his grandparents' farm near Wapakoneta, Ohio. As a teenager Neil had many interests, including playing jazz saxophone, but his obsession was flying. He began to take flying lessons when he was 14 years old, and he received his pilot's license on his 16th birthday. When he left high school in 1947, Armstrong entered a local university to study aircraft engineering as an air cadet in the U.S. Navy. The

The mighty Saturn V rocket clears the launch pad carrying the Apollo 11 crew on the first leg of their journey to the moon.

outbreak of the Korean war in 1950 meant that Armstrong was called to active service. He flew 78 combat missions and was awarded three medals.

After the end of the war in 1953, Armstrong returned to his university and completed his studies. When he graduated in 1955, he enrolled as a civilian research pilot working for the government. During the next seven years, he tested some of the fastest aircraft ever built, piloting them at speeds of over 3,600 miles (6,000 km) per hour. In 1962, inspired by President Kennedy's intention to win the Space Race, Neil Armstrong volunteered to train as an astronaut, and was accepted.

His first flight was aboard the Gemini 8 vehicle that performed the first successful piloted space-docking (see page 26). An engine failed during the final part of the flight, but Armstrong managed to stabilize the Gemini vehicle so that it survived reentry. Afterwards, there was considerable praise for his "extraordinary piloting skill," and when crews were being selected for individual stages of the program, Armstrong was assigned to Apollo 11. Later, Neil Armstrong was chosen to be the first human being in history to step on the moon.

The flight of Apollo 11

Moon

On July 16, 1969, the Saturn V rocket carrying Apollo 11 was launched from Cape Canaveral.

The first two stages of the rocket separated after their fuel was exhausted, but the third stage containing the Apollo vehicle went into orbit around the Earth. After several orbits, the third-stage rockets fired again, this time in the direction of the moon. After their fuel was used up, the third stage separated, leaving Apollo 11 to continue alone, driven by the rockets in the service module.

The route of the Apollo 11 mission.

Launch

Landing

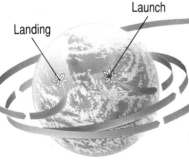

Earth

After three days traveling through space, Apollo 11 went into orbit around the moon. Armstrong and Aldrin transferred to the landing module, leaving Collins aboard the command module. The landing module, which had been named "Eagle," then separated and descended to make a perfect soft landing near an area of the moon called the Sea of Tranquillity. The first words sent back to Earth from the moon were "Tranquillity Base here. The Eagle has landed." Apollo 11 had arrived safely on the moon on July 20, 1969.

One small step

After carrying out some essential checks, the astronauts put on the gloves and helmets of their spacesuits and their life-support system backpacks. They opened the door of the landing module. Neil Armstrong went through, and climbed down the short ladder. As he reached the bottom and made the first human footprint on the moon's surface, he uttered the most famous speech ever made by an explorer: "That's one small step for a man, one giant leap for mankind."

Aldrin soon joined Armstrong, and the two astronauts practiced walking on the moon. Together they carried out experiments, collecting samples of moon rock, and taking scientific measurements. After spending almost two and a half hours on the moon's surface, they returned to the landing module. About 12 hours later they fired the rockets that lifted them back into lunar orbit. Besides their footprints, the astronauts left behind them scientific instruments, a commemorative plaque, an American flag, and the lower part of the lunar module.

After space-docking with the rest of the Apollo vehicle, they transferred back to the command module and rejoined Michael Collins. They then fired the rockets in the service module to start their return journey to Earth. As the spacecraft approached Earth, the service module separated, and only the command module reentered the Earth's atmosphere. The command module splashed down in the Pacific Ocean, and the astronauts were quickly picked up by helicopters from waiting ships. The first journey to the moon had been successfully completed.

After their return to Earth, Armstrong and his fellow astronauts were bundled into an "isolation-tank" in case they had picked up any moon-germs during the trip. Eighteen days later, when the doctors were finally satisfied that there were no germs, the astronauts emerged to meet the world. Everybody wanted to see in person the astronauts they had watched on television. After parades through three American cities, they went on a world tour visiting 22 different countries. None of the three astronauts has visited space again.

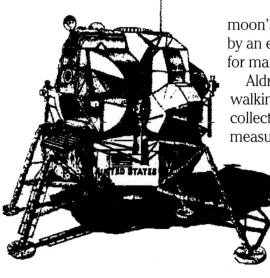

The landing module "Eagle" on the moon.

The impact left by Armstrong's first step will remain undisturbed in the lunar dust for millions of years.

Astronaut "Buzz" Aldrin stands beside the American flag. The flag was stiffened with wire because there is no wind on the moon to make it flutter.

Discoveries and Achievements

Space pioneers

Until Yuri Gagarin made his historic flight, many basic questions about space remained unanswered. How, for example, would a person react to the increased force of gravity as a rocket sped away from the Earth? Would a person be able to operate equipment in conditions of weightlessness? Could a person survive the reentry of a space vehicle through the Earth's atmosphere? Gagarin's historic space flight answered these and many other questions. His journey of discovery showed that it was possible for people to travel into space.

When Neil Armstrong first walked on the moon, he extended the scope of human exploration and discovery to include new worlds in space. Before the success of Apollo 11, nobody could be certain that the exploration of other planets was possible.

Gagarin and Armstrong are justly famous, not least for their courage in braving the unknown. However, it must be remembered that their voyages of discovery were only possible because of the work of thousands of other people. Armstrong's journey to the moon required eight years' work by a team of some 300,000 scientists, engineers, and technicians. Although a smaller team had sent Gagarin into space back in 1961, the Soviet space research organization expanded during the 1960s to rival that of the Americans in size.

It must also be remembered that space exploration was not without risk. In January 1967, three American astronauts were killed when their Apollo command module caught fire during a pre-launch exercise. In April of the same year, the first Russian Soyuz vehicle to be launched crashed after reentering the Earth's atmosphere, killing the cosmonaut aboard. During the 1970s and '80s, space exploration cost more lives.

Views of the Soviet (above) and American (right) control rooms show the large number of people involved on the ground in space projects, and the close similarity of displays and equipment used by the two superpowers.

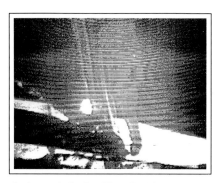

Grainy and obtained by television cameras outside the lander, the picture shows Neil Armstrong taking his historic "giant leap" onto the moon.

A giant leap

Neil Armstrong's first words on the moon were extremely well chosen. The success of Apollo 11 did indeed represent a "giant leap." In less than 30 years, from September 1939 to July 1969, the world had leapt forward from piston-engined aircraft to rocket-powered space vehicles.

This "giant leap" began with World War II. But not all of the technology involved in the moon landing had its origins in military purposes. The years of peace during the Cold War allowed the development of other technologies. To many people, the most amazing part of the whole expedition to the moon was that they watched it on television. After opening the door to the landing module, the first thing Neil Armstrong did before climbing down the steps to the surface of the moon was to switch on the television cameras mounted on the outside of the module. The television pictures were transmitted to Earth, and then rebroadcast via orbiting satellites. As a result, more than half a billion people sitting in their homes or crowded around shop windows in the street watched and listened as the first man stepped onto the moon.

Eyes in the sky

Satellites were one of the first successes of the Space Race. Specially equipped communications satellites could "bounce" television signals from one part of the Earth to another. The first communications satellite, Telstar, was launched by the United States in 1962. For the first time, a television audience in one country could watch events as they happened in another part of the world, thousands of miles away. By the end of the 1960s, there were more than a dozen communications satellites in orbit around the world, and television via satellite had become commonplace.

Communications satellites were not the only satellites to be launched during the 1960s. Other satellites carried cameras and different types of sensors to obtain information about the Earth. Satellite photographs showed every detail of the Earth's surface and could be used for making maps, or planning roads and harbors.

Communications satellites orbiting the Earth relay telephone and television signals around the world.

Photographs taken with special filters and film could show whether crops were healthy or ready for harvesting.

Cameras aboard satellites could also photograph the cloud formations associated with storms and hurricanes. Other sensors

A natural-light image (right) of the San Francisco Bay area taken from the Landsat satellite. Built-up areas appear gray. A detail of the San Francisco image (below) which has been computer-colored to provide more information. Buildings and roads are pale blue, and vegetation is colored red.

could measure temperatures in the lower atmosphere. Using information from satellites, scientists were able to obtain a better understanding of how the world's climates operate. Improved weather forecasting is just one of the benefits obtained from these "eyes in the sky."

Some satellites were launched to help ships navigate at sea. These satellites made two orbits of Earth per day, at a height of about 11,000 miles (18,000 km). Equipment installed aboard ships could use signals from these satellites to establish the ship's position on the Earth's surface extremely accurately.

Satellites were also sent out from the Earth to probe space and to orbit around other planets. These "space probes" carried much the same sort of equipment as the satellites in Earth orbit. At the same time as Armstrong was setting foot on the moon, the American Mariner 7 probe was sending back detailed photographs of the surface of Mars.

An overhead view of buildings in Washington, D.C. This photo was taken from orbit by a Russian spy satellite.

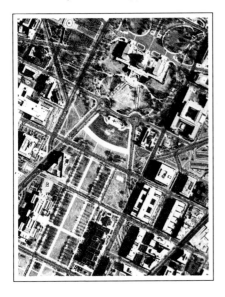

Features on the surface of Mars, photographed by Mariner 7 in July 1969.

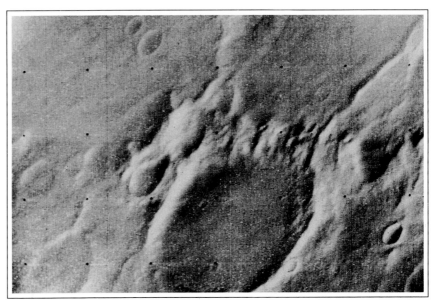

Technological spin-offs

Today, it is easy to forget how much of a boost the Space Race gave to the development of technology during the 1960s. The goal of being first on the moon meant that huge amounts of money were spent on research and development. Not only did the scientists and engineers have to design new equipment, they also had to make it small enough and dependable enough to travel to the moon and back.

Much of the equipment that was developed and produced for the lunar expedition also had other uses. Some items were immediately made available to the public. The most famous were the lightweight "space blankets," used to keep people warm in an emergency. These are manufactured from a mirrored plastic that was developed as an insulation material for spacesuits. Innovations such as the space blanket are called "spin-offs" from the Space Race.

The most important spin-offs, however, were not as immediately obvious. These were the advances in making miniature electronic equipment, especially computers, to fit inside a space vehicle. In solving the problems presented by the Space Race, electronic engineers made huge advances that would eventually benefit everybody. Less than two years after the Apollo 11 lunar landing, the first pocket calculators were produced. Since then, an electronic revolution has transformed the way people live and work.

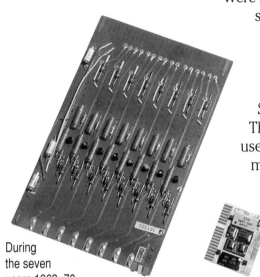

During the seven years 1963–70, electronic components reduced in size by more than 500 percent. The smaller circuit board shown here (made in 1970) does exactly the same as the larger board (made in 1963).

The classic view of our planet from space, a world rich in liquid water and atmospheric oxygen produced by living plants.

A new world view

One of the most important achievements of the Space Race was one of the least expected. The photographs of the Earth taken during the voyages to the moon, and from the moon's surface, provided people with a new image of their planet. For the first time they were able to see their planet as it was—a brightly colored jewel revolving in space. They could see the whole of the Earth, the blue oceans, the green forests, and the white clouds that carry life-giving water around our world.

The view from space, combined with the information sent back by space probes, showed that Earth was a very special place. The moon and the other planets showed absolutely no signs of life, no matter how closely scientists looked. Only on Earth was there the right balance of sunlight, water, and air that makes life possible in all its marvelous variety.

Space and the Lunar Environment

Conditions in space

Space begins at the upper edge of the atmosphere, officially defined as being 60 miles (100 km) above the Earth's surface. Beyond the Earth's atmosphere, space is a hostile environment.

There is no air in space. Instead there is a complete emptiness that is called a vacuum. On Earth, a vacuum can only be produced by special laboratory equipment and can only exist inside a sealed container. In space the situation is reversed; everywhere is a vacuum, and air can only exist inside sealed containers. However, providing air for people to breathe in space is only part of the problem. Inside a vacuum there is no atmospheric pressure (see page 15). So in space, human beings do not just need oxygen; they also need a securely pressurized environment.

Space itself is very cold—at -454°F(-270°C) it is about three times colder than the coldest place on Earth. Space is cold because it is an empty vacuum. Objects in space, when they are in shadow, will also be extremely cold. However, when they are in sunlight, the same objects will rapidly gain heat and become much hotter than temperatures on Earth.

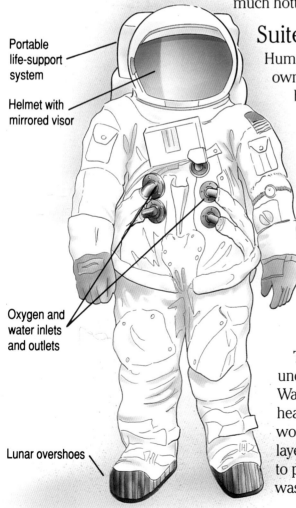

An *Apollo* spacesuit.

Portable life-support system

Helmet with mirrored visor

Oxygen and water inlets and outlets

Lunar overshoes

Suited to space

Human explorers in space have to be provided with their own separate environment in which there is oxygen to breathe, and the air pressure and temperature are controlled. The equipment used to provide this environment is known as a life-support system. In a space vehicle, this system is attached to the crew compartment so that the whole compartment is maintained as a suitable environment for humans. Inside the compartment, the crew do not need any special clothing or equipment. But in order to venture outside the vehicle, for a spacewalk or on the moon, each member of the crew must wear a special suit with its own portable life-support system. In addition to protecting the occupant from the hazards of space, a spacesuit must also allow him or her to move around easily.

The spacesuits worn on the moon had a lightweight undergarment that contained a network of plastic tubes. Water circulating through these tubes carried away body heat and kept the wearer pleasantly cool. Over this was worn a bulkier outer garment that was made of several layers of artificial fiber. This outer garment was reinforced to provide some protection against tiny meteoroids, and was insulated against extremes of temperature. Gloves, boots, and helmet were all tightly sealed in place so that the whole suit could be pressurized. Oxygen and water were circulated through the suit from the portable life-support system, which was worn on the back.

The space-helmets were in three parts. A cloth headset carried communications equipment. Over this was an inner pressure helmet that was made of a single piece of transparent plastic. The outer helmet protected the inner helmet from damage, and was fitted with a darkened and mirrored visor to shield the wearer's eyes from strong sunlight.

Together, the suit and equipment weighed a total of 176 pounds (80 kg), a heavy load that made walking extremely hard work—on Earth. On the moon, where the force of gravity is much lower, the suit "weighed" less than 33 pounds (15 kg), so movement was much easier.

Electricity, Food, and Water

Aboard space vehicles, electricity to power radio and other equipment is provided by powerful batteries or by fuel cells that combine hydrogen and oxygen. But satellites and space stations usually generate their own electricity by using energy from the sun. Sunlight can be turned directly into electricity by devices called solar panels. On Earth, where sunlight is filtered by the atmosphere, solar panels are mainly used to power small items such as calculators and watches. In space, without the filtering effect of the atmosphere, solar panels work much more efficiently and can provide a continuous supply of electricity.

An American astronaut chases the last of his sandwich in midair.

Conditions of weightlessness in space present strange problems for eating and drinking. Food will not stay on a plate, and water simply floats out of cups. Food and drink has to be sealed into plastic containers so that space travelers can suck the contents through a tube. Washing is even more difficult. Special shower units have been constructed that use a strong current of air to suck the water downward, producing conditions similar to those on Earth.

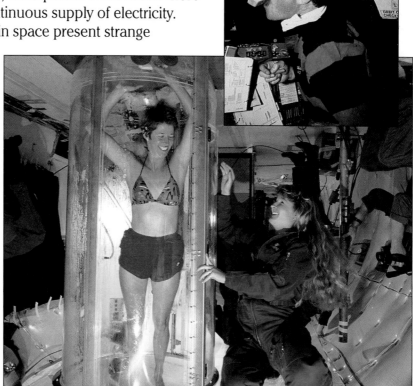

An astronaut taking a prototype space shower, for use in weightless conditions.

On the moon

The moon turns on its axis much more slowly than the Earth, and a lunar "day" lasts nearly 28 of our days. There are almost two weeks of sunlight, followed by an equal period of complete darkness. In sunlight, the temperature on the moon's surface rises to above 212°F (100°C). During the long lunar night, temperatures fall to about -241°F (-155°C). Water cannot exist under these conditions, and as well as being airless, the moon is also dry.

Although the lunar landscape often looks gently rounded from a distance, up close the rocks can be seen to be every bit as rough and jagged as those on Earth.

Much of the moon's surface is composed of regolith, a layer of broken and crushed rock about 66 feet (20 m) deep. In most places, there is a layer of fine dust on top of the regolith. This dust layer can be up to 12 inches (30 cm) thick. Because there is no atmosphere, there is no weather on the moon. Without any wind or rain to disturb the surface, the footprints left in the lunar dust by human explorers will remain there for many thousands, if not millions, of years.

Like the Earth, the moon's surface is not completely flat. There are areas of highland and lowland, and there are even mountains and valleys. However, the moon's surface is dominated by a series of features that are very rare on Earth—meteorite craters.

Many millions of years ago, the moon was bombarded by thousands of meteorites coming from space. As each meteorite struck, it "splashed" out a circular crater, like a pebble thrown into a pool of thick mud. Some of the meteorites must have been huge, because they created craters hundreds of miles in diameter, although most are smaller. There is usually a steep-sided ring wall around the edge of a moon crater. The mountain ranges on the moon, some of which are thousands of feet high, are the remains of huge ring walls that have almost been obliterated by further meteorite bombardment. The inside of a crater is often completely flat and covered with dust. But some craters have peaks of highland in the center, formed when rocks "bounced" back after the initial impact.

A few recently formed craters are marked by highly visible rays radiating out from the ring wall. These rays are made of pale-colored rock that was splashed out by the impact. The most famous ray crater is named Copernicus, after the astronomer. The Copernicus crater was formed about 800 million years ago, and it is easily seen through a small telescope or binoculars.

Large lowland areas of the moon are almost free of craters, and have a smooth dark appearance. These features are known as *maria* which means "seas." These lunar "seas" are the remains of huge ancient craters that have become filled with lava (molten rock) seeping up from inside the moon. Some of the smaller craters have dark floors, which suggests that they too are filled with solidified lava.

The presence of lava on the moon led some scientists to believe

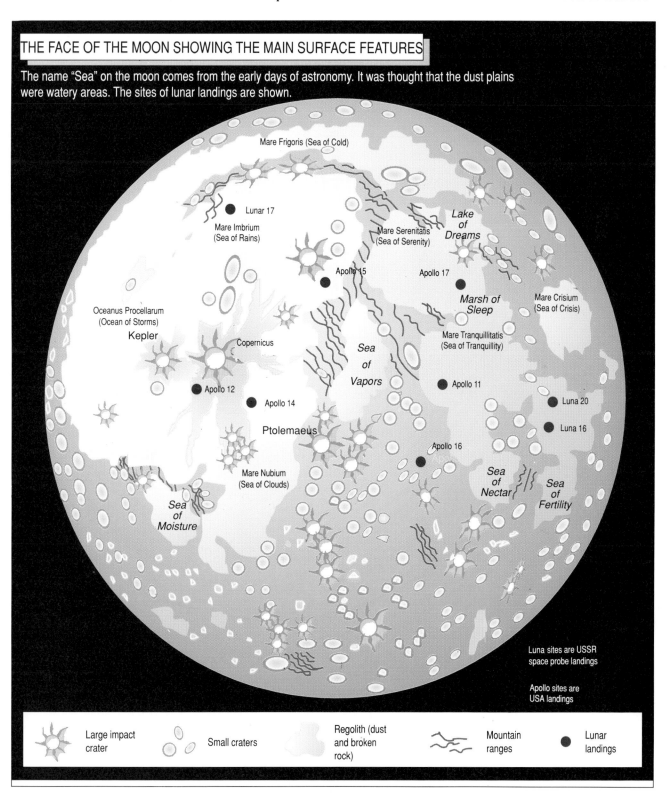

that some of the craters might be the remains of lunar volcanoes. But although this remains a possibility, and molten lava may glow on the moon's surface, all the evidence suggests that the moon has no volcanoes. However, there are "moonquakes," similar to earthquakes. Moonquakes may have created the huge cracks or valleys that are found on the moon. These cracks are known as rills.

Two close-up photos of the surface of Venus, taken by the Russian Venera 13 vehicle, the only craft that has so far functioned on the hostile surface of this planet.

Venus

Although human explorers have not yet reached any other planets, scientists have sent robot space probes to gather information. Venus is the nearest planet to Earth, and almost exactly the same size, but the similarity ends there.

Venus has a very thick atmosphere that consists almost entirely of unbreathable carbon dioxide. The clouds in Venus's atmosphere are made up of sulphuric acid, which dissolves living things and most metals. Because the atmosphere is so thick, the atmospheric pressure is very high—about 90 times higher than Earth's. A person standing on the surface of Venus would be squashed flat immediately. In 1982, the Soviet probe

An image of the landscape of Venus produced by the American Magellan radar mapping probe. In the background is a five-mile- (8-km-) high volcano with lava flowing from its sides.

Venera 13 made a successful soft landing on Venus and sent back the first color pictures of its barren, rocky surface. Instruments aboard the probe showed that the temperature at the surface was 869°F (465°C), much too hot for water or living things to exist. During 1989, the American probe Magellan orbited Venus and used radar to produce a map of the surface. The Magellan probe discovered that Venus had huge volcanoes, though none have been active recently.

The surface of Mars photographed by a Viking Lander. Part of the Lander is visible in the foreground, and this has allowed scientists to assess the color of the red Martian soil.

Mars

Mars is the next closest planet to Earth, and in many ways it is similar to our planet. Mars has a thin atmosphere, which is mostly carbon dioxide.

Space probes orbiting Mars have photographed huge valleys and canyons, much larger than any seen on Earth. These were made by rivers, millions of years ago, before most of Mars's water evaporated into space. Mars is now almost completely dry, although there are small patches of water ice at the north and south poles, and fog occasionally forms in lowland areas. The photographs also showed that Mars has the highest mountain yet discovered, a huge, ancient volcano that rises more than 16 miles (26 km) above the surrounding plain.

In 1976, America sent two Viking probes to land on Mars. Pictures from the Viking probes showed that Mars was a barren, dusty, rocky world where temperatures rarely rose above 59°F (15°C), and could fall as low as -148°F (-100°C). The probes took samples of Martian soil and conducted experiments, but they found absolutely no sign of life on the planet. As far as we know, the only life in the universe is here on planet Earth.

Space Talk

The human exploration of space has produced its own vocabulary. Some of these "words" are actually sets of initials. If you read more about space exploration, you may come across the following:
NASA—North American Space Administration, the U.S. organization responsible for space exploration.
Mission Control—the NASA spaceflight control center in Houston, Texas.
CAPCOM—Capsule Communicator, the person in Houston who communicates with space vehicles.
DOI—Descent Orbit Insertion, the flight of the Lunar Module from orbit to the moon's surface.
LRV—Lunar Roving Vehicle, a moon-buggy.
PLSS—Portable Life-Support System.
EVA—Extra Vehicular Activity, a spacewalk.
EMU—Extravehicular Mobility Unit, a suit for working in space.

What Happened Later

Good-bye to the moon

Between 1969 and 1972 the United States sent five more Apollo vehicles to the moon, and in total a dozen people have walked or driven on the moon. On some of the later visits, astronauts made use of "moon-buggies" with electric motors, a strong lightweight framework, and special wheels that were adapted to the lunar surface. These moon-buggies allowed the astronauts to explore and collect samples over a much larger area than before. In 1972, the U.S. stopped sending people or probes to the moon. The scientists had decided that, for the time being, they had learned all that they needed to know about Earth's satellite.

The LRV "moon-buggy" enabled astronauts to explore a much larger area of the moon than was possible on foot.

The USSR never succeeded in landing a person on the moon, and this remains a uniquely American achievement. However, Soviet scientists did succeed in bringing their own samples of moon rocks back to Earth. In 1970, a Soviet probe soft-landed on the moon, collected samples, and fired them back to Earth in a rocket capsule. Later the same year, a Soviet robot moon-buggy was landed on the moon's surface. Under remote control from Earth, this robot traveled over the lunar surface for several months, sending back pictures and other information.

The next steps

The American landing on the moon did nothing to lessen the rivalry between the two superpowers, and the United States and the USSR continued their separate exploration of space.

At first, the Americans concentrated on sending long-distance probes to the more distant planets and beyond. In 1972, they launched Pioneer 10, which was boosted to a record-breaking 30,000 miles (50,000 km) per hour as it left Earth's gravity. One year and nine months later, Pioneer 10 reached its target and sent back the first close-range pictures of Jupiter. Other probes have since been launched, most notably Voyager 1 and Voyager 2. These probes sent back the first high-quality images of the planets Saturn, Uranus, and Neptune.

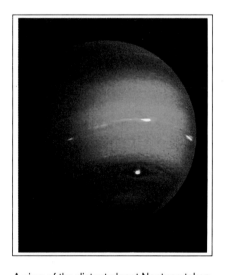

A view of the distant planet Neptune taken by the Voyager probe. The red color is due to haze in Neptune's atmosphere. The white streaks are high-altitude clouds. The temperature on Neptune is about -382°F (-230°C).

Soviet scientists concentrated on perfecting techniques for docking vehicles, and for living and working in space. Cosmonauts stayed in orbit longer and longer, and progressively larger space vehicles were launched. In 1971, the Soviet Union launched Salyut, the first permanently orbiting "space station." Salyut was maintained in rotation by teams of cosmonauts. In 1973, the United States launched a similar space station named Skylab.

Other nations also began to take part in space exploration, building their own scientific satellites. Some launched their own satellites, but most had to be placed in orbit by Russian or American rockets. Meanwhile, U.S. scientists were developing a revolutionary new idea for getting in and out of Earth orbit—the space shuttle.

The First Spaceship

Shaped like a stubby jet aircraft, the American space shuttle was the world's first reusable space vehicle—the first true spaceship. The shuttle can carry eight astronauts and 30 tons of payload. It was first launched in 1981, and it was a great success. In 1986, however, a tragedy occurred. The shuttle *Challenger* exploded shortly after being launched, killing all seven astronauts on board. Shuttle flights were halted while experts investigated the cause.

After the problem was identified and solved, the shuttle went back into service. Since then the shuttle has carried dozens of people and many tons of cargo into space, including the Hubble Space Telescope. The Soviet Union has also built a shuttle craft that looks very similar to the American design.

The American space shuttle was the world's first reusable spacecraft. Launched vertically with rocket boosters (above), it lands like an aircraft after reentering the Earth's atmosphere (right).

Political rivalry

Whatever the results of the Space Race, relations between the two superpowers remained distinctly unfriendly throughout the 1960s, 1970s, and 1980s. Each accused the other of trying to expand its influence and interfere in the affairs of smaller nations, and both were guilty. From time to time, efforts were made to bring about a more peaceful relationship between the U.S. and the USSR. During the mid-1970s, there was talk of "détente" between the superpowers. Détente means "better relations." For a while there was hope, and the improved relationship was marked in space when American and Soviet space vehicles docked for the first time in July 1975.

Despite this small success, the superpower rivalry continued. During the 1980s the Americans made plans for a space defense system to shoot down Soviet missiles. These plans became known as "star wars" because of the advanced technology that was to be employed. But before the star wars project could ever be put to the test, the situation changed dramatically. At the end of the 1980s, the Soviet empire, and the Soviet Union itself, began to crumble and collapse.

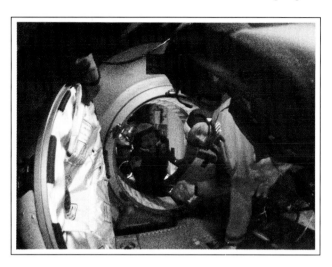

Handshake in space — cosmonaut and astronaut link hands after Soviet and U.S. spacecraft dock for the first time as part of the process of détente.

The collapse of the Soviet system

The Soviet system had never been completely stable. The non-Russian parts of the Soviet Union had always resented being dominated by Russians, but the power of the secret police prevented any organized opposition. The countries that formed the Soviet empire in Eastern Europe had been discontented ever since 1945. In several countries, such as Hungary in 1948 and Czechoslovakia in 1968, there were attempts to break free from the Soviet system. Each time, Russian soldiers were sent to crush the opposition and enforce Soviet power. However, the Russian soldiers could not remove the desire for freedom. During the 1980s, anti-Soviet feelings increased. In Poland a non-Communist workers' movement named "Solidarity" was formed.

In 1987, the Soviet leadership announced a series of limited reforms—there was to be greater political freedom to criticize the system, and people were to have greater economic freedom to run their own businesses. These reforms also applied to the occupied countries in Eastern Europe. One of the reforms was the right to free elections.

In June 1989, the Polish people rejected the Communist Party and elected Solidarity to form a new government. In September, Hungary opened its borders, allowing people to move freely across the Iron Curtain. In November, the German people began to dismantle the Berlin Wall. By the beginning of 1990, the Soviet empire in Europe was no more. The Communists had been

The flag of the Solidarity Movement.

For 30 years the Berlin Wall divided the city in two. Tearing the Wall down marked the symbolic end of Communist rule in Europe.

removed from power by freely elected governments.

During the early 1990s, a similar chain of events followed in the Soviet Union. Some of the non-Russian states in the USSR declared their independence and others followed. Some wished to remain linked to Russia economically, while others wanted complete independence. By the beginning of 1992, the Soviet Union was no more, and the Communist Party had lost control, even in Russia itself. The Cold War was over, and there was now only one superpower—the United States.

The fact that the Soviet system failed in the end does not take anything away from some of the Soviets' achievements, especially in the fields of science and space research. The Soviet space station Mir, launched in 1986, survived the transfer of power and remained in orbit. Cosmonauts aboard Mir hold several space records, including those for endurance. Crew members have spent more than 300 consecutive days in weightless conditions before returning safely to Earth.

Working in space

Living and working in space for up to a year at a time is now a reality, and this opens up many new opportunities. In the weightless conditions aboard a space station, some chemical substances do not behave in the same way as they do on Earth.

The EMU (extra-vehicular maneuvering unit) enables astronauts to maneuver themselves in open space, leading the way to the construction of large space stations in orbit.

Miniature factories aboard shuttles and space stations have already produced high-quality drugs and electronic equipment that are difficult, if not impossible, to make on Earth.

People can also work in open space. Since 1984, American astronauts have been using powered backpacks to propel themselves around in space. Wearing these backpacks, astronauts can maneuver freely to move large pieces of equipment into position. The next space stations will be constructed in space by the astronauts themselves.

The story of the first steps into space marks the end for the time being of the story of human exploration. During the last 1,000 years, human beings have traveled a long way. Who knows where we might travel in the future?

Glossary

astronomer Someone who studies objects in space.

atmospheric pressure The weight of air, or other gases, above a planet's surface.

atomic bomb (A-bomb) An explosive device that operates by the atomic fission of uranium or plutonium.

booster A detachable rocket engine used to assist the launch of a larger rocket.

capsule A small space vehicle carrying no more than three crew members.

Cold War The mutual hostility and suspicion that existed between the United States and the Soviet Union between 1945 and 1990.

collective farm A state-owned and operated farm in a Communist country.

Communist Someone who follows the political theory that all economic activity should be carried out by the state.

gravity The attracting force that is a property of mass.

hydrogen bomb (H-bomb) An explosive device that operates by fusion of hydrogen, also called a nuclear or thermonuclear bomb.

life-support system The equipment that maintains a suitable environment around people in space.

meteor A bright streak of light in the sky caused by a particle of dust from space, also called a shooting star.

meteorite A lump of rock or metal from space that hits the surface of a planet or moon.

meteoroid A dust particle, or lump of rock or metal, traveling through space.

moon A natural satellite. Earth's natural satellite is the moon.

orbit The path of one object around another in space.

orbital velocity The speed of an object in orbit.

rocket An engine that operates by the thrust of exhaust gases.

satellite An object that orbits around a planet. Astronomers distinguish between natural satellites (such as Earth's moon), and artifical satellites launched into space by human beings.

soft landing The arrival of a space vehicle on the surface of a satellite or planet without damage to the crew or instruments aboard the vehicle.

Soviet Union A political superpower created by enforced joining together of independent countries after the Russian Revolution of 1917. The Soviet Union was dominated by Russia for more than 70 years, but the Union began to fall apart in 1990.

Space Race The struggle between the United States and the Soviet Union to be the first to explore space and develop space technology.

space shuttle The reusable space vehicle developed by the United States.

spacewalk To leave a space vehicle and venture into space protected only by a spacesuit.

superpower A country that has sufficient economic and military strength to dominate a large part of the world.

treaty An agreement between two or more countries.

vacuum Space that contains nothing.

weightlessness The condition of floating in zero gravity that is experienced in space.

Further Reading

Armbruster, Ann and Taylor, Elizabeth A. *Astronaut Training*. Franklin Watts, 1990

Asimov, Isaac and Giraud, Robert. *The Future in Space*. Gareth Stevens, 1993

Baker, D. *Danger on Apollo Thirteen*. Rourke, 1988

Biel, Timothy L. *The Challenger*. Lucent Bks., 1990

Briggs, Carole S. *Women in Space: Reaching the Last Frontier*. Lerner, 1988

Cross, Wilbur. *Space Shuttle*. Childrens Press, 1987

DeOld, Alan R. and Judge, Joseph W. *Space Travel: A Technological Frontier*. Delmar, 1990

Dolan, Terrance. *Probing Deep Space*. Chelsea House, 1993

Embury, Barbara and Crouch, Tom D. *The Dream Is Alive: A Flight of Discovery Aboard the Space Shuttle*. Harper Collins, 1991

Furniss, Tim. *The First Men on the Moon*. Franklin Watts, 1989

Graham, Ian. *Space Science*, "Facing the Future" series. Raintree Steck-Vaughn, 1992

Hawkes, Nigel. *Into Space*. Franklin Watts, 1993

——— *Space Shuttle*. Franklin Watts, 1990

Herda, D. J. *Operation Rescue: Satellite Maintenance and Repair*. Franklin Watts, 1990

Ridpath, Ian. *Space*. Franklin Watts, 1991

Spangenburg, Ray and Moser, Diane. *Space People from A to Z*. Facts on File, 1990

Sullivan, George. *Day We Walked on the Moon: A Photo History of Space Exploration*. Scholastic, 1990

Vogt, Gregory. *Apollo and the Moon Landing*. Millbrook Press, 1991

——— *The Space Shuttle*. Millbrook Press, 1991

Westman, Paul. *Neil Armstrong: Space Pioneer*. Lerner, 1980

Index